MODERN STARS

CYNTHIA ERIVO

by Alexis Popi

Essential Library

An Imprint of Abdo Publishing

abdobooks.com

ABDOBOOKS.COM

Published by Abdo Publishing, a division of ABDO, PO Box 398166, Minneapolis, Minnesota 55439.

Printed in China.
102025
012026

Cover Photo: Daniele Venturelli/Getty Images for The Red Sea International Film Festival/Getty Images Entertainment/Getty Images
Interior Photos: Bruce Glikas/FilmMagic/Getty Images, 5; Jenny Anderson/Getty Images, 8; Walter McBride/WireImage/Getty Images, 11, 42; Theo Wargo/Getty Images for Tony Awards Productions/Getty Images, 13; Robert Gauthier/Los Angeles Times/Getty Images, 14; ZGPhotography/Shutterstock Images, 17; PA Wire/AP Images, 19; Walter McBride/Getty Images, 20; Mike Kemp/In Pictures/Getty Images, 22; Arnold Turner/Getty Images for NAACP/Getty Images, 25; Shutterstock Images, 26; Nobby Clark/Popperfoto/Getty Images, 29; Wirestock Creators/Shutterstock Images, 31; John Phillips/UK Press/Getty Images, 35; Volodymyr TVERDOKHLIB/Shutterstock Images, 36; Stuart Monk/Shutterstock Images, 39; Lifestyle Pictures/Alamy, 45; Kevin Winter/SHJ2018/Getty Images for TIFF/Getty Images, 47; Horatio Seymour Squyer/Wikimedia Commons, 49; Entertainment Pictures/Alamy, 52; Kevin Winter/Getty Images, 55; Gilbert Carrasquillo/WireImage/Getty Images, 57; dpa/AP Images, 59; Ben Gabbe/Getty Images for Hearst/Getty Images, 61; Kevin Winter/Getty Images for NARAS/Getty Images, 64; Cindy Ord/Getty Images for Tory Burch/Getty Images, 67; Lia Toby/Getty Images, 69; Frazer Harrison/Getty Images, 70; Album/Alamy, 73; FlixPix/Alamy, 76; Stefanie Keenan/Getty Images for FIJI Water/Getty Images, 78; Rich Polk/Penske Media/Getty Images, 82; Leon Bennett/Getty Images for ESSENCE/Getty Images, 85; Amy Sussman/Getty Images, 88; Jeff Spicer/Getty Images, 91; Matt Winkelmeyer/Getty Images for GLAAD/Getty Images, 93; Marleen Moise/Getty Images, 94; Scott Garfitt/BAFTA/Getty Images, 99

Editor: Riley Madsen
Series Designer: Karli Hughes

Library of Congress Control Number: 2025939222

PUBLISHER'S CATALOGING-IN-PUBLICATION DATA

Names: Popi, Alexis, author.
Title: Cynthia Erivo / by Alexis Popi
Description: Minneapolis, Minnesota: Abdo Publishing, 2026 | Series: Modern stars | Includes online resources and index.
Identifiers: ISBN 9781098298104 (lib. bdg.) | ISBN 9798384931904 (ebook)
Subjects: LCSH: Erivo, Cynthia, 1987- --Juvenile literature. | Theatrical actors--Biography --Juvenile literature. | Motion picture actors and actresses--United States--Biography--Juvenile literature. | African American motion picture actors and actresses--Biography--Juvenile literature.
Classification: DDC 792.64--dc23

CONTENTS

CHAPTER ONE

REACHING FOR THE SPOTLIGHT

When 29-year-old British actress and singer Cynthia Erivo woke up on the morning of June 12, 2016, she felt excited but nervous. For the first time in her life, she had been nominated for one of the most prestigious awards in stage acting: a Tony Award for Best Leading Actress in a Musical. She was being recognized for her performance as Celie in a revival of *The Color Purple* at the Bernard B. Jacobs Theatre on Broadway in New York City. The musical is based on the 1982 Pulitzer Prize–winning novel of the same name by Alice Walker.

Celie is among the most complex and emotionally draining but rewarding characters in *The Color Purple*

Erivo's performance in a revival of *The Color Purple* brought her to new levels of fame. >>

to embody. She is a young Black woman who is constantly ridiculed for her looks. She survives rape by her stepfather, is married off to an abusive husband, and is later forcefully separated from her children. She endures this trauma by writing letters to her sister in Africa, with the hope of one day reuniting with her.

"I never thought Celie was an ugly girl," said Erivo. "She might be small, the runt of the family, the one who's running around constantly, who hasn't had time to look at herself in the mirror. But I think she's lovely. And toward the end [of the show], she sees that about herself."[1]

Since Erivo's move to New York City from London, England, in 2015, she had been hoping to make a name for herself in the theater world, a community full of talented people also trying to make their mark. With seemingly endless

A PRIZE-WINNING NOVEL

***The Color Purple*, a novel by Alice Walker, was published in 1982. The book won a Pulitzer Prize in 1983, making Walker the first Black woman to win the prize in fiction. The novel was praised for spotlighting strong female characters and giving them a voice. "I think in any book, you choose your main characters, and the main characters in this novel are Celie, Shug and Nettie, and it is about the bonding of women," Walker said at the time. "And these are women for whom men are not central. I say of myself and I say of them that men are not the center of my universe; I am the center of my universe."[2]**

auditions and meetings with casting directors, it was a challenging existence but one Erivo knew she was cut out for. When she landed the role of Celie, Erivo had a hunch that the experience would change her life forever.

NONSTOP PRESS

In the weeks leading up to the Tony Awards at the Beacon Theatre in New York City, Erivo did everything she could to stay calm. She ran every morning, maintained a healthy diet, and tried to get enough sleep. In addition to her eight shows a week on Broadway, she also did interviews with reporters from all over the country about her Tony nomination.

In one interview with a New York City news channel, Erivo expressed her love for the stage and her deep gratitude for all the praise she had received. "There are so many people that want to do that, that want to be on stage and want to perform in front of people . . . as someone who's done it and this is their very first time . . . I just feel really, really lucky," she said. "I just hope that anyone who's starting out knows that anything is possible."[3]

On May 23, less than a month before the awards ceremony, Erivo also performed one of the songs from

Erivo, *front right*, and costar Jennifer Hudson, *front left*, received applause from the audience after the opening-night performance of *The Color Purple*.

The Color Purple, "I'm Here," on *The Late Show with Stephen Colbert*. This was the same song she would eventually perform at the Tonys. Decked out in a stunning black dress and accompanied by a full orchestra in the back of the stage, she belted out the ballad with such power and emotion that it brought tears to the eyes of many people in the audience. When the song was over, the crowd gave her a resounding standing ovation.

Erivo wasn't sure her talent and soaring voice would be enough to win a Tony over her competitors. Other women in the lead actress category included Phillipa Soo, who played Eliza Hamilton in *Hamilton*; Jessie Mueller, who played Jenna in *Waitress*; Laura Benanti, who played Amalia Balash in *She Loves Me*; and Carmen Cusack, who played Alice Murphy in *Bright Star.* Still, as the days inched closer, Erivo felt more confident than ever that her success onstage was only just beginning.

ANOTHER STANDING OVATION

Erivo and other cast members from *The Color Purple* performed "I'm Here" at the Tony Awards. The number was introduced by Oprah Winfrey, who referenced the play's long journey from novel to movie to stage, saying, "As it does for everybody who experiences it, this new production succeeds in stunning, in surprising, and in catapulting us to our feet as if it were completely new."[4] At the end of Erivo's final note, the audience erupted in applause. Once again, nearly every person in the theater cheered, giving Erivo yet another standing ovation.

THE BIG NIGHT

When Erivo arrived at the Beacon Theatre on the evening of June 12, 2016, the red-carpet festivities were already in full swing. The air buzzed with excitement as reporters milled about, trying to capture special moments with as many actresses and actors as possible. Dressed in a stylish black tuxedo, *Hamilton*'s Lin-Manuel Miranda stood in front of the cameras as photographers snapped photos. Other Tony Award nominees, including Lupita Nyong'o, Sophie Okonedo, Michelle Williams, Daveed Diggs, and Jonathan Groff, stood by and smiled, waiting their turn to be featured in the spotlight. High-profile presenters, such as Uzo Aduba, Cate Blanchett, Common, Neil Patrick Harris, and Jake Gyllenhaal, appeared on the red carpet as well.

When it was her turn to be interviewed, Erivo seemed relatively relaxed. She smiled wide and did a twirl in front of the camera to show off her dress. She also answered questions about the bond she felt with Celie in *The Color Purple*. "[Celie] is, I guess, a mix of vulnerability and

AN EYE-CATCHING LOOK

When Erivo attended the 2016 Tony Awards, she made an impression with more than just her incredible voice. She was decked out in an eye-catching, multicolored, ruffled gown made by esteemed fashion designer Roberto Cavalli. The dress had cutouts in the sides. On her feet, Erivo wore a pair of Art Deco–inspired sandals by luxury brand Salvatore Ferragamo.

Scott Sanders, lead producer of *The Color Purple*, joined Erivo on the red carpet at the 2016 Tony Awards.

strength all at once," she said. "I love playing her because she's able to spread a message of self-love and being able to forgive and being a strong person in one's self. It takes a while for her to realize it, but she gets there in the end, and I think it's the getting there that's the most important thing."[5]

"I don't believe that many things are impossible to achieve so long as you put your mind to it and take the time to get it done."[7]

—Cynthia Erivo, 2017

In those moments before the ceremony, Erivo did indeed feel relaxed. But just a few hours later, when the award for Best Leading Actress in a Musical was being presented, her nerves got the better of her. As actress Audra McDonald came to the front of the stage and read off the nominees, Erivo held her breath. When Erivo's name was called as the winner, her mother, who was sitting next to her, gave her a giant kiss on the cheek. Erivo looked down at her lap, then up at the camera with a gigantic grin.

She walked to the stage, careful not to step on her dress, held up her Tony Award, and said, "Hi, Mummy. Look!" Then she thanked Oprah Winfrey and the rest of the show's producers, Alice Walker, and everyone in the cast who shared the stage with her.

"To every single person in my cast, you are magnificent," Erivo exclaimed with tears in her eyes. "Thank you so much for lifting me up when I'm tired, for holding my hand when I'm happy, for kissing me on my forehead when you know I just need some love . . . everyone in that theater, thank you."[6]

In her acceptance speech, Erivo thanked other members of the cast of *The Color Purple* by name.

Across her career, Erivo has entertained audiences in a variety of art forms.

A LEGEND IN THE MAKING

Erivo won her first major award for singing and acting in 2016, but it wouldn't be her last. In fact, over the next decade, she would go on to be nominated for or win other prestigious honors too, including a Grammy, an Emmy, and an Oscar. Following her first starring role as Celie, she would play other emotionally complex leading women, including real-life figures such as Harriet Tubman and Aretha Franklin. And she would learn to sing while flying through the air as one of literature's most beloved villains, Elphaba, the Wicked Witch of the West, in the movie adaptations of Gregory Maguire's novel *Wicked*.

From her humble roots in London to her journey to the United States to pursue a career in acting, and from her work as a solo musician to her status as an icon of fashion and style, Erivo is determined to succeed in every task she takes on. She's come a long way since performing one of her first solos in a primary school play back in London.

"That little kid was bitten by the bug immediately after singing that song," she said in a 2024 interview. "I learned that there was a certain power in being able to make people feel. And I wanted to keep doing that."[8]

CHAPTER TWO

A STAR IS BORN

Cynthia Chinasaokwu Onyedinmanasu Amarachukwu Owezuke Echimino Erivo was born on January 8, 1987, in South London, England. Her mother, Edith, and her father immigrated to England from Nigeria when Edith was 24. When Cynthia was young, her parents divorced, and her father moved out. She saw him occasionally, but her mother largely raised Cynthia and Cynthia's younger sister, Stephanie, on her own.

Cynthia often wondered about her parents' marriage and why they divorced. Still, her childhood was full of love and support. Her mother worked as a nurse. She taught new mothers parenting skills

Although she no longer lives in London, Erivo occasionally returns to visit family members. >>

and made sure they weren't suffering from postpartum depression, a mood disorder involving loss of appetite, insomnia, and ongoing feelings of sadness, hopelessness, and anxiety. Edith also worked directly with newborns and kids up to three years old, teaching them cognitive and behavioral skills.

A STRONG ROLE MODEL

From the time Cynthia was a girl, she looked up to her mother as a role model. Even though Edith was busy raising two children and holding down a job, she still did everything she could to make sure her girls had a comfortable life. In interviews, Cynthia has talked about how growing up in an all-female household enabled her to be the strong, independent woman she is today. She said, "Often the world tells us [Black women] that we aren't able to do certain things but when all you know is other women doing everything they want to, you realize, yeah I can too."[1]

After school, Cynthia loved to stage recitals for her mother and sister, sing Aretha Franklin and Diana Ross songs, and dance around the house. When she was five years old, she gave her first public performance in front of a large audience. She sang the Christmas carol "Silent Night" at a school holiday pageant. She remembers feeling inspired by the positive reaction of people in the audience, including her mother.

Aside from singing, young Cynthia had other talents. She attended secondary school at the La Retraite Roman

Diana Ross, *right*, was a member of the Supremes, a girl group that became famous in the 1960s.

Catholic Girls' School and did well in her studies. She excelled at playing the clarinet, the saxophone, and the viola. She was a conductor for her church choir. And she performed as Fagin in a school production of *Oliver!* when the older student who was originally cast backed out of the role. Cynthia's drama teacher, Andrea Masoliver, recalled how Cynthia's singing impressed audiences.

When Cynthia was 11, she auditioned for and got a part in a local stage production of Bertolt Brecht's *The Caucasian Chalk Circle*. At 15, she landed her first big role as Juliet in *Romeo and Juliet* as part of a youth outreach program at the Young Vic, a venue in London's West

Erivo's mother often attends her daughter's performances and award ceremonies.

End neighborhood. She also appeared on *Trust Me, I'm a Teenager*, a British reality show in which teens gave advice to people and tried to solve their problems. By that point, Cynthia had gotten a taste of what it meant to be a performer.

AN UNEXPECTED LOSS

At 16, Cynthia was trying to sing and act as much as she could. At home and at school, she felt as cherished and as self-assured as ever. But one day, when she and her father were standing in the middle of a London tube station waiting for the next train to arrive, an unexpected event occurred that nearly crushed her usually confident demeanor.

Seemingly out of the blue, Cynthia's father told her he no longer wanted to be a part of her life or her mother's and sister's lives. Instead of just being divorced from her mother, he wanted to be permanently gone. "I didn't see it coming because, you know, what 16-year-old would?" Cynthia later told National Public Radio (NPR). "At the time, I was heartbroken, because it was in public when it happened as well. . . . And I think I felt bad for having to have to bring that information back to my house, to my mom and my sister."[2]

After the shattering news, Cynthia's father stuck to his word. He didn't call or write. He effectively vanished from his former family's lives for good. Her father's abandonment took a long time for Cynthia to process. "I never really compartmentalized it. I just saw someone doing something that hurt me. And I think it was just

Theatre Royal Stratford East in London opened in 1884.

sort of as simple as that, like, someone is—he was doing something that he knew would hurt me to be mean and spiteful," she said. "But I knew that he was going to stick to it. I knew that it wasn't, like, a jab that he would take back at some point."[3]

SWITCHING COURSE IN COLLEGE

Still reeling from the sudden absence of her dad, Cynthia tried to move on and make the best of her life. She threw herself into performing. During the rest of her time in high school, she starred in a number of school productions, including *Guys and Dolls*, *Annie*, and *My Fair Lady*.

After graduating high school, she applied to college at the University of East London. At the time, she didn't realize she could major in acting, so she studied music psychology instead. When she had time amid her schoolwork, she sang at local bars and clubs.

But a year into her studies, Cynthia grew bored with her major and dropped out. She went to work as an usher at the bar within Theatre Royal Stratford East. She hoped this would be a way to get her foot in the door of the professional theater world but was shocked when she was repeatedly denied an audition.

"I just thought: 'If I'm in a theater, maybe there's a chance, I could meet a director, I might just meet somebody,'" she said. "You don't realize until you're working in a theater that there's a weird division—an invisible line comes up. You think you're in this hub but you aren't."[4]

As fate would have it, a former mentor stepped in. Artistic director Rae Macken, who had cast Cynthia as Juliet in *Romeo and Juliet* when she was 15, was teaching an acting course at Stratford East. When Cynthia asked

A MISSED OPPORTUNITY

In 2007, the same year she was accepted to RADA, Cynthia auditioned to be a backup singer for the Irish boy band Westlife. She nailed the audition and was given the job. The money would have gone a long way to helping her pay for school. Unfortunately, RADA wouldn't allow it. She was forced to decline the gig because it would mean missing the first two weeks of classes. Looking back on this experience in a 2025 interview, she said that the administrators at RADA did not understand how to work with students who did not come from a lot of money.

to join, Macken said she would let Cynthia train only if she applied to the Royal Academy of Dramatic Art (RADA), the most prestigious performance arts university in England.

At first, Cynthia refused to apply, doubting that she would be accepted. Eventually, she relented. When she auditioned in 2007, she was formally accepted.

TRAINING WITH THE BEST

For the next three years at RADA, Cynthia studied with the best of the best. Although she learned a lot, much of the time she spent there was challenging. Many of her classmates came from much wealthier backgrounds than she did.

On top of her studies, she worked as a seamstress for shirtmaker Thomas Pink to pay for her schooling. "I genuinely had to work much harder than other students, and I got penalized for it. I'd come in exhausted, and they'd say: 'Well, she's not dedicated. She's not concentrating.' It took me a long time to make people understand that I wasn't lazy—I was just tired," she said.[5]

Although she adored reading August Wilson plays in class and learning how to breathe correctly when singing Stephen Sondheim songs, she also didn't land many parts. She auditioned repeatedly and tried to support her fellow classmates, but she was cast only in small roles.

"First, it was because they thought I wasn't concentrating. It was like a punishment. The second time,

Although the time she spent at RADA was challenging, Erivo says that graduating from the school was an invaluable step in her career.

RADA was founded in 1904. Over the years, it has opened several facilities across London.

I can't even remember the excuse. The third year, the excuse was, they thought I was 'efficient' and other people needed more help," she said.[6]

She also faced discrimination because of her race. "She'd had a lot of experience, and was very confident in a class of very white English that didn't appreciate that coming from someone else," said Dee Cannon, an acting coach at RADA who worked with Cynthia. "That's an English problem, but it became a Cynthia problem."[7]

In her third and final year, Cynthia grew so exasperated by not being given a chance to show her talent that she put on her own cabaret for the public. It was here that an agent saw her perform and asked to represent her. When she graduated from RADA in 2010, Cynthia felt ready to make her mark on the world. Despite all the heartache, she had gotten what she needed from her schooling.

A CULTURAL TOUCHSTONE

When Cynthia attended RADA, she read and reread the work of August Wilson, a revered, Pulitzer Prize–winning Black playwright. Wilson is best known for his collection of ten plays called *The Pittsburgh Cycle* that chronicle the Black experience in the 1900s. After his death in 2005, he became the first Black playwright to have a Broadway theater named after him.

She said, "I think I'm just so grateful, and you take the good with the bad. Learning what I needed to learn at RADA meant that I could learn what I needed to learn in theatre, and learning what I learned in theatre meant I knew what to do on Broadway, and that's set me up for TV and film."[8]

CHAPTER THREE

CLIMBING THE ROPES

After graduating from RADA, Erivo was determined to pursue a career in show business. She went to countless auditions, hung out with theater people, and tried to stay on top of any new shows originating in or traveling to London. All that hard work paid off. From 2010 to 2014, she landed a series of roles on some of England's most popular theater circuits.

Her first stage role was in *Marine Parade* at the Brighton Festival, a large event that includes dance, theater, music, and circus performances throughout Brighton and Sussex, England. Her first musical role was in *I Was Looking at the Ceiling and Then I Saw the Sky* at Theatre Royal Stratford East. In 2011, she

Dress rehearsals for *The Color Purple* took place ahead of the show's opening night on July 15, 2013. >>

portrayed Deloris Van Cartier in a UK tour of *Sister Act*, a stage musical adaptation of the 1992 movie starring Whoopi Goldberg. A year later, in December 2012, Erivo appeared in *Living Every Day*, which was staged as part of a celebrity gala in London's West End.

A NEW IMAGE

When Erivo attended RADA, she often hid behind her shoulder-length hair, even when she was performing onstage. But after she graduated, she decided it was time to let her true personality shine and cut off all her hair. At first, her hairdresser wouldn't do it and gave Erivo only a trim. A week later, Erivo returned to the salon, demanding a fully shaved head. She loved how emboldened her new bald head made her feel. "Being powerful is every day finding what the most authentic version of yourself is that day and sticking with it, not allowing other people's perception of who you are or what you are sway you," she said.[1]

Even though she was cast in plenty of stage parts, Erivo didn't exactly have an easy time of it. Preparing for auditions and dealing with rejections was hard. She also rarely got called back for screen work, something she had wanted to break into for a long time. Despite her thick British accent, some casting agents and directors assumed she wasn't even from England.

BIG BREAK

In 2013, Erivo auditioned for the role of Celie in a production of *The Color Purple*. This version was a

The Menier Chocolate Factory Theatre opened in 2004. The original factory had been built in the 1870s.

precursor to the one that opened on Broadway in 2015. It was put on by the Menier Chocolate Factory, a theater inside an old chocolate factory building. At the time, she was acting at the Soho Theatre in London in the musical *Lift*, and the show was about to close. She didn't like having too much time between jobs.

"Celie is a role that I have dreamed of playing since I was 10," she told theater critic Jonathan Baz in an interview at the time. "It is one of the most rounded roles ever written for a Black female . . . either in theatre or in film, and I love the grit that's in her character."[2]

Within days of her audition, Erivo received word that she had gotten the part. She was overjoyed by the news. From the minute she joined the cast, she memorized lines, perfected her southern American accent, and practiced tirelessly until she got the part right. When the time came to perform, Erivo put her heart and soul into making Celie come alive for the audience.

"ANYTHING WORTH HOLDING ON TO"

About halfway through the run of *The Color Purple*, famous New York composer Scott Alan flew to London to do a one-night show with a star-studded cast full of famous singers. He asked Erivo to perform "Anything Worth Holding On To," an autobiographical song he had written about his struggles with depression. Erivo cried when she sang it, and the audience loved it.

For two months, in a small theater that seated about 200 people, Erivo performed eight shows a week. In the early shows, she worried that she would lose hold of the character. But she managed to remind herself to remain consistent in playing Celie.

Despite getting a standing ovation on opening night and on many nights thereafter, Erivo found the process of becoming a character who was constantly criticized and abused draining. During one performance, she had a breakdown onstage. She tried to say her lines, but all she could do was cry. "It was really challenging. I had to figure out a way to process it every day," she said in a BBC interview. "We did . . . over 300 performances. You're called ugly every day. After night 100, the line between you and the character becomes very, very thin. It doesn't feel like the character. It feels like you."[3]

Still, the audience adored her and the show. Some even stamped their feet and shouted encouragement as Celie found her inner strength and learned how to stand up for herself. Critics loved Erivo's performance too. *The Guardian* gave her a very positive review, and Erivo was nominated for Best Actress in a Musical at the WhatsOnStage (WOS) Awards.

"DIMINUTIVE POWERHOUSE"

In 2014, after the success of *The Color Purple*, Erivo was riding high. Since that show was so exhausting, she decided to switch gears by auditioning for a comedy. In February, she was cast as Chenice in *I Can't Sing!*, a musical co-produced by Simon Cowell. Her performance led her to be described as a "diminutive powerhouse."[4] The play parodied *The X Factor*, a TV show in which singers

A DATE WITH THE QUEEN

On February 17, 2014, celebrities gathered at London's Buckingham Palace for a lavish gala to celebrate Queen Elizabeth's 60-year support of RADA. Helen Mirren recited a speech from *The Tempest*. Jessie Buckley played Eliza Doolittle in a scene from George Bernard Shaw's *Pygmalion*. And Cynthia Erivo sang a song from *The Color Purple*. Ten years later, in May 2024, King Charles and Queen Camilla visited RADA to get a tour and learn more about the school's productions. Erivo, who was elected as the school's vice president in 2024, showed them around.

across England, Northern Ireland, Wales, and Scotland competed to be crowned the next singing sensation. "It has been incredibly technical for me, as well as being a combination of great fun and phenomenally hard work," Erivo said of the experience. "I am not a quintessentially funny comedy actress, so I have really enjoyed discovering my comedy timing."[5]

When the time came for *I Can't Sing!* to go live, audiences flocked to see Erivo perform. But for some people, it didn't live up to the hype. The show got mixed reviews and closed just a little more than six weeks after it opened. Undeterred, Erivo continued to audition for other parts.

From July to August 2014, she starred in the European premiere of *Dessa Rose* at London's Trafalgar Studios. Though she didn't win, her performance as the character

Simon Cowell, *second from left*, is known for serving as a judge on talent competition shows such as *American Idol* and *The X Factor*.

Dessa earned her a nomination as Best Leading Actress in a Musical at the BroadwayWorld UK Awards. In the fall, she got the lead role in the twentieth-anniversary rendition of *Songs for a New World* at the St. James Theatre.

By the end of the year, Erivo's career was steadily moving upward. It was then that she received startling news, something she hadn't imagined in her wildest dreams would come true. Nearly a year before, after

Broadway is located in Manhattan, one of New York City's five boroughs.

opening night of *The Color Purple*, one of the show's producers had asked her what she thought about taking the show to Broadway in New York City. At the time, Erivo was sure he was kidding.

But her producer wasn't joking. In fact, toward the end of the year, when a Broadway theater agreed to host the play, Erivo was formally asked if she would play Celie in the United States. The thought of leaving her family, friends, and everything she knew behind to go live in a new country made Erivo feel incredibly nervous. Up until the last minute, she didn't know if she'd have the courage to go through with it. On the morning of her flight to the United States, she even left a bunch of clothes in her drawers in case she'd need to come back.

When Erivo got to the airport, she started crying and almost didn't get on the plane. In a later interview, she recalled struggling with the fact that leaving for New York would mean leaving behind her life in London. It was the scariest decision she had made in her life thus far.

But Erivo swallowed her fear and got on the plane. On the long flight to greet her new life in New York, she reflected on all the choices she had made to get her to that point. She took a deep breath and braced herself for whatever daunting but hopefully thrilling adventures would come next.

CHAPTER FOUR

A BIG MOVE PAYS OFF

In 2015, at 28 years old, Erivo arrived in the United States to take the next step in her career. In addition to Erivo as Celie, *The Color Purple* featured Jennifer Hudson as Shug Avery and Danielle Brooks as Sofia. From the minute rehearsals began, Erivo felt close with her cast members, who both admired and supported her as she adjusted to her new life in New York. Hudson, for example, praised the quality of her singing and her perseverance as a performer.

Despite the camaraderie with her fellow actresses and actors, life in New York wasn't always exhilarating for Erivo. In fact, trying to navigate New York City's bustling city streets and learn the customs of a new

The many theaters located on Broadway in New York City have made the street the center of American theater. >>

BROADWAY
SNOW ROUTE
NO STANDING
DURING
EMERGENCY
VEHICLES TOWED

“I feel like it is changing my life. . . . Every step of the way, every day something new comes along with new people I meet, new things, new experiences, and I think it’s helping me grow as an actress.”[2]

—Cynthia Erivo, 2015

country while adapting to a new show made her feel quite bewildered at first.

She struggled with her confidence at times, not just onstage but outside of work too. “When you’re on your own by yourself, having to figure out this new place in a new show where nobody knows you . . . it just was these huge, massive stages that I had to figure out that had both joy in it but real loneliness sometimes because I just had never experienced it,” she said.[1]

MAKING IT ON BROADWAY

Eventually, adjusting to life in New York City got easier. For more than one year, Erivo performed in *The Color Purple* at the Bernard B. Jacobs Theater, often to sold-out audiences. This time was thrilling but arduous.

To keep her mind clear and body fit, she started running around her neighborhood in Brooklyn. The more she ran, the more focused and fit she became. “I have eight shows a week. It’s extremely physical. In my role as Celie, I rarely leave the stage over the course of two-and-a-half hours. There are fights and dancing and it's a workout every time you get on stage," she said. "Being physical outside of work allows me to have the stamina to do that. There are days when your mind is tired and the only thing that can get you through is your body."[3]

Despite Erivo's occasional exhaustion, it never showed onstage. She received nearly universal praise for her performance. Reviews from major publications rolled in.

TRAINING TO WIN

Erivo started running at 22 when attending RADA. During the Broadway-revival run of *The Color Purple*, she ran to keep her stress levels down, even on the days when she had two shows to perform. She became so interested in running that she started training for the New York City Marathon. On November 6, 2016, Erivo completed the New York City Marathon in 3 hours, 57 minutes, and 7 seconds.[5] She credits her interest in distance running with teaching her the lesson of patience.

One reporter from the *Los Angeles Times* wrote, "Front and center is the London-trained Cynthia Erivo as Celie. . . . Relatively unheralded, she brings stark humanity—and an astonishing voice—to the role. . . . It's hard to imagine that Erivo's heart-stirring Broadway debut, a portrayal that derives enormous power from humility, won't be recognized once award season arrives."[4] A reporter from the *New York Times* agreed, writing, "Ms. Erivo's sobering and stirring portrayal of Celie, in a

Members of the cast of *The Color Purple* celebrated the musical's soundtrack at a listening party on February 11, 2016.

rapturously reviewed revival of a musical version of *The Color Purple* . . . [has] brought the kind of praise that can change a performer's career."[6]

And change Erivo's career it did. *The Color Purple* ran for more than 400 performances from November 10, 2015, to January 8, 2017. Erivo won several awards, including the 2016 Tony Award for Best Actress in a Musical. Erivo and the cast of *The Color Purple* won the Daytime Creative Arts Emmy Award in the category of Outstanding Musical Performance in a Daytime Program for an appearance they made on *The Today Show*. The show's soundtrack also won Best Musical Theater Album at the 2017 Grammys.

Throughout all the glitz and glamour, Erivo felt grateful for the chance to share her talent with the world. "I didn't know that it held so much gifting in it, whether it be discovering what kind of actress I could be or discovering the depth I could find onstage or just being able to have doors open that I didn't think would be open to me," she revealed in an interview on *CBS Mornings*. "It's been a wonderful experience to be able to play this character in this role on Broadway for the first time."[7]

A MOVE TO FILM

After her sweeping success on Broadway, Erivo decided not to return to London. She made the United States her home. To scratch that persistent itch of becoming a screen actress, she moved to Los Angeles, California, to pursue a career in film.

Up until that point, Erivo had only a few on-screen credits to her name. Her first had been an episode of the British sitcom *Chewing Gum* in 2015. A year later, she followed with small appearances on the drama series *Mr. Selfridge* and *The Tunnel*. But after *The Color Purple* closed and Erivo moved to Los Angeles, it seemed every director in town wanted to work with her.

She made her film debut in 2018 in the thriller *Bad Times at the El Royale*. The film follows a group of strangers staying at the seedy El Royale Hotel in the late 1960s. Over the course of the film, stolen money, political paranoia, and murder turn the hotel's residents against one another. Each character's secrets are revealed before a final shocking and violent conclusion.

EGOT

In the entertainment world, very few people have achieved EGOT status. This means winning major awards for work in four different entertainment fields: an Emmy for television, a Grammy for music, an Oscar for film, and a Tony for Broadway theater. By 2017, Erivo was on her way to becoming the youngest member of the club by winning an Emmy, Grammy, and Tony for her performance in *The Color Purple*. All she needed was an Oscar. Through 2025, only 21 people had achieved this status, including Whoopi Goldberg and Jennifer Hudson.[9]

Critics loved Erivo's performance as the sneaky, conniving Darlene, a down-on-her-luck singer trying to find her next big break. "Erivo supplies much of the soundtrack in beautiful, haunting stripped-down covers of '60s classics," wrote one reporter from the website *Collider*. "She gives a musical tour-de-force, as Darlene's voice is her power, weakness, and salvation all at once."[8]

That same year, Erivo was cast in a smaller role in another thriller called *Widows*, an action-packed revenge film starring Viola Davis. Adapted from a 1983 British miniseries, the movie chronicles what happens during a heist performed by three women, who team up after their

Erivo's costars in *Bad Times at the El Royale* included Jon Hamm, *left*, and Lewis Pullman, *center*.

criminal husbands are killed by a gang for stealing from them. Erivo plays a hairstylist named Belle. In a few pivotal scenes, she joins the three women in stealing money from a mansion. Though the movie did not sell very many tickets and was largely passed over for awards, critics once again praised Erivo.

In her new home, Erivo didn't limit herself to just film. In the summer of 2019, Erivo produced and starred in the seven-part, scripted science-fiction thriller podcast *Carrier*. She voiced the lead role of Raylene Watts, a Black long-haul truck driver transporting a trailer with mysterious contents. The podcast's creator, Dan Blank, said he wanted to focus on how Black women made up only a small fraction of truck drivers on the road.

A LEARNING CURVE

As an actress, Erivo was used to performing onstage in front of a live audience. But when it came to working on films, she had a lot to learn. In *Widows*, which was shot before *Bad Times at the El Royale* but released later, she realized she needed to be bigger on set. "Your vocal presence has to be a little bit bigger than I thought in my head," she said in an interview. "And it took me some time to get used to seeing myself onscreen. I'll watch it once and then it'll freak me out for a little bit, and I'll need to take some time away from something and then watch it again."[11]

"There are some people whose imaginations open widely when you're singing them a song or telling them a story, and they don't necessarily have to see the picture in front of them to imagine something," Erivo said of the experience. "So, I think I just wanted to be a part of that world, really. It's intriguing. And it's still acting in a way. I'm as physical as I would normally be, as emotionally invested as I would normally be on stage in front of people."[10]

Erivo was pleased with her first few forays into show business on the silver screen and in podcasts. She had achieved more than she had ever imagined, and her career was slowly but surely inching forward. But even bigger on-screen appearances were yet to come.

Erivo attended the premiere of *Widows* on September 8, 2018, in Toronto, Canada.

CHAPTER FIVE

TWO KNOCKOUT ROLES

By the fall of 2019, Erivo was already making waves in Hollywood after her Tony, Grammy, and Emmy wins for *The Color Purple*. One person who was especially impressed with the British actress was Debra Martin Chase. She was the producer of *Harriet*, a much-anticipated biopic about Harriet Tubman, the heroic American abolitionist who escaped slavery and led more than 70 enslaved people to freedom.

Chase chose Erivo for the lead role after seeing her knockout performance in *The Color Purple*. *Harriet* was scheduled for nationwide release in November 2019, and no one was more excited for it to come out than Erivo.

Harriet Tubman is remembered as one of the most prominent leaders of the abolitionist movement. >>

But the process of making *Harriet* had not been easy. From the first spark of inspiration in the 1990s to the film's release on November 1, 2019, the journey was riddled with bumps and obstacles. Gregory Allen Howard wrote the screenplay in the mid-1990s. But he faced significant pushback in getting the movie made. Hollywood executives told him that nobody would pay to see a movie about enslaved people.

Decades passed before the environment in Hollywood changed. Howard credits the viral social movement #OscarsSoWhite, as well as the major success of films such as *12 Years a Slave* and *Hidden Figures*, a movie based on the true story of three trailblazing Black women at the National Aeronautics and Space Administration (NASA), for making *Harriet* possible.

#OSCARSSOWHITE

In 2015, about 92 percent of directors of the 100 top-grossing Hollywood films were men. Eighty-six percent of those films featured white actors or actresses in the leading roles. On January 15, 2015, when the Oscars nominations were announced, the Academy of Motion Picture Arts and Sciences had given all 20 nominations for acting to white people.[1] The same thing happened the following year. The phenomenon inspired lawyer April Reign to create the social media hashtag #OscarsSoWhite, which sparked a worldwide movement and call for more representation for women and people of color in Hollywood.

In 2016, development of the movie finally began. But the film took a while to take shape. Some of the people scheduled to work on it had opposing ideas about how it should be made.

Seith Mann, the film's original director, was ultimately replaced with Kasi Lemmons because of creative differences. "He was talking about a very violent and visceral version of the film, which I'm sure would have been an incredible version in its own right," said coproducer Daniela Taplin Lundberg. "When Kasi came in and talked about the film, it was a film of inspiration, and a film about a *woman* as much as a hero."[2]

Another issue concerned the decision to cast Erivo as Harriet. When word got out that a British actress would play the celebrated American, some members of the public were furious and took out their frustration on social media. They fired off posts claiming Erivo stole the part from more deserving Black American actresses. Some people even called her prejudiced against Black Americans.

> **"I'm stubborn. I kept asking if we were ready, if we were going to get there, if it was going to get made. I was sure it was going to happen."**[3]
>
> **—Cynthia Erivo, 2019, on the production of *Harriet***

Erivo's cast members ignored the criticism and

Erivo says that playing Harriet Tubman changed her life.

stood by Erivo from beginning to end. "Cynthia has continued to lead that sort of charge with all the grace and dignity and courage that she took on the role of Harriet with," said Erivo's costar Leslie Odom Jr. "She ain't afraid of nuttin' out here! Cynthia is a liberated Black woman. She gonna do what she wants to do, you know what I mean?"[4]

A REWARDING JOURNEY

Despite the backlash she faced on social media during the filming of *Harriet*, Erivo did what she knew best: she threw herself into fully embodying her character. She read everything she could about Tubman's life and legacy. She took voices lessons from a dialect coach to learn how to speak in a lower register and in an 1840s Maryland accent. And she sang along with gospel records, imitating Tubman's habit of singing.

As Tubman was a deeply religious woman, Erivo also reconnected with her faith and sometimes prayed with members of the cast on set. "To understand her faith and courage, I needed to probe my own faith and call on it. Harriet never did anything without listening to God for guidance, being present to the dangers she faced and present to what could take her through them," Erivo said. "It was such an honor to portray her, but I couldn't have done it without my faith."[5]

By the time the cast and crew were finished filming, Erivo was once again drained. She went back to

A TOUCHSTONE FROM CHILDHOOD

To prepare for playing Tubman, Erivo dipped back into her childhood to remember the central role faith played in her upbringing. In fact, it was her mother who introduced Erivo to religion. "We prayed over dinner, and she heard my bedtime prayers. I also heard her pray in the shower and in the bathroom when she was getting dressed before work. She prayed out loud, talking to God as though he was right there in the room with her. There were no restrictions when it came to prayer. You could pray at any time and all times. God was with you," Erivo said.[6]

London for a quick trip and collapsed from physical and emotional exhaustion.

"In the middle of the night, my body shut down—I got really ill out of nowhere. . . . I felt like I was drowning," she said of that time. It was only with a good, long cry that she was able to feel better. "Having the release was important," she said. "Because I think it was the first time I had let go."[7]

In early 2020, a few months after *Harriet*'s release, Erivo was nominated for several awards. They included two Golden Globes and a Critics' Choice Award. Other nominations rolled in from Black Entertainment Television (BET) and the National Association for the Advancement of Colored People (NAACP).

She also received two Oscar nominations: one for Best Performance by an Actress in a Leading Role and another for Best Original Song for cowriting and performing the movie's lead track, "Stand Up," which Erivo sang at the awards ceremony. Erivo brought her mother to the Academy Awards show. Although she didn't end up winning either award, Erivo was overjoyed by the experience. She expressed gratitude for being able to perform at the Oscars and for being nominated for two awards.

The lyrics of "Stand Up" contain themes of freedom and sacrifice, themes which also appear in *Harriet*.

THE QUEEN OF SOUL

Erivo had come a long way since the days of auditioning for television spots in London and not landing a part. With roles like Celie and Harriet Tubman propelling her toward stardom, it seemed nothing could stop her from achieving her dreams. In 2020, she starred as private investigator Holly Gibney in the HBO miniseries *The Outsider*, a television adaptation of the Stephen King novel of the same name.

The role was originally intended by King to be a white woman but was recast as a Black woman at the urging of producer and costar Jason Bateman, who wanted the chance to work with Erivo. That same year, she launched her own production company called Edith's Daughter, named after her mother. The company's goal was to invest in projects devoted to telling the stories of overlooked and underrepresented people.

With the start of 2021, Erivo's prospects kept on getting better and her schedule busier. In March, she wowed TV audiences by playing the part of Aretha Franklin in *Genius: Aretha*, a standalone series on National Geographic. It all started when she was on the red carpet during her entrance to the 2019 Tony Awards. A reporter had asked her to name her guilty-pleasure song and she responded by singing a bit of Franklin's "Ain't No Way."

Unbeknownst to her, the interview got sent to the show's producers, Clive Davis and Brian Grazer. Not long after the red-carpet interview aired, her agent called to tell her the show's producers wanted to cast her as Franklin. Erivo agreed immediately. She described Franklin as an inspiration for her singing and as a hero of hers.

As usual, Erivo trained for the part by watching every interview and performance with Franklin she could find. She played every record she could get her hands on too. She listened to them on repeat, trying to learn how

Erivo sang at a 2018 tribute show for Aretha Franklin following the legendary singer's death.

to breathe as Franklin did when singing. "I would have to listen over and over again, just to catch the breaths that she would do, the breaks, the way she would move from one note to the other."[8]

The series finally aired on television in March 2021, a year later than originally planned due to delays related to the COVID-19 pandemic. Erivo felt overwhelmed with gratitude at the chance of being able to embody such a legendary musician. In an interview, she discussed the challenge of portraying Franklin's professional and personal life, saying that the role required a lot of preparation for her to feel ready.

Once again, Erivo was nominated for many awards for her performance, including a Critics' Choice Television Award, an Emmy, a Golden Globe, an NAACP Image

MEETING ARETHA

For Erivo, playing the Queen of Soul was the chance of a lifetime. So was meeting the legendary singer in person. Erivo first met Franklin when Franklin came to see *The Color Purple*. After the performance, the 73-year-old Franklin came backstage and sang a line from "I'm Here" to Erivo and then complimented Erivo's own singing. A year later, the two stars bumped into each other again, this time at the Kennedy Center in Washington, DC. During a performance, Erivo sang "The Impossible Dream" as part of a star-studded cast. Franklin, sitting in the audience, sang along with her eyes closed.

Critics have called Aretha Franklin the greatest singer in American history.

Award, and a Screen Actors Guild (SAG) Award, but she did not win any of them. Erivo didn't let those losses slow her down. By the spring of 2021, she wasn't just thinking about her acting career. Always a singer, she was also working toward achieving another dream: making a record of her own.

CHAPTER SIX

BRANCHING OUT

After the success of *Genius: Aretha* in the spring of 2021, Erivo's career was going as well as it ever had. Her schedule for the future was packed. Even Oprah Winfrey noticed the fledgling star's busy schedule and sent Erivo a note suggesting the actress should avoid overtaxing herself. "I will never forget getting that email," Erivo said in an interview. "I'm glad it meant that she was paying attention to what was going on in my life, which meant that she cared. So that's cool. It's cool when Oprah Winfrey cares about you."[1]

But like the rest of the world in 2020 and 2021, Erivo struggled emotionally during the COVID-19

Oprah Winfrey played a role in keeping Erivo in the cast of *The Color Purple* after its move to Broadway. >>

pandemic, when many people saw their loved ones and colleagues less often. "I did feel really lonely. I remember I was in LA [Los Angeles] on my own . . . I had loads of people around me, but I felt like I was doing my life solo, and it was going really fast at that time," she said. "I was sort of like in the middle of what felt like a storm. And I felt like I was just by myself and I just didn't know how to really handle it completely."[2]

SAGE ADVICE

Throughout her life, Erivo has always paid tribute to the women who have inspired her along the way. When she was playing Aretha Franklin, she thought a lot about what the Queen of Soul taught her. "The most important lesson I learned from Aretha was probably perseverance, strength, and determination," Erivo said in an interview with *Harper's Bazaar UK*. "She knew what she was worth and fought for it."[3]

Instead of wallowing, Erivo started a creative project she had always wanted to complete but never had enough time to devote her energy to. Working on *Genius: Aretha* had given her the courage to take chances and explore who she really was as a singer. Now she wanted to put her musical talent to work and create a solo album.

"Learning Aretha's story and what she had been through gave me a boost of confidence with my own music," Erivo said. "I felt empowered to do the things I wanted to. I wasn't afraid to say, 'I don't like that, I think we should do that again.' And learning her songs forced me to learn my own instrument. I discovered that there were [new] sounds and riffs I could do."[4]

Writing her own lyrics and composing her own songs taught Erivo more than she expected about being a musician and remaining true to herself. "A lot of these songs are really personal. So, I'm ready to share something about me and my life and who I am," she said. "It's like another part of my life I get to sort of see come to fruition. I've been wanting to do an album for a very long time."[5]

A DEBUT RECORD

By the time Erivo finished writing and rewriting sets of lyrics and putting them to music, she had nearly 40 songs to choose from. After listening and relistening to each song, she whittled down the list to the final 12 tracks and gave the album a name: *Ch. 1 Vs. 1.* She also enlisted the help of Harold Lilly, who had produced music for Beyoncé; Jack Splash, who produced for Alicia Keys; and executive producer Will Wells, whose clients included Barbra Streisand and Quincy Jones.

"From reworking the song to then making the record to then checking in with each other during the mix, to even the mastering process, she was deeply involved,"

Erivo and singer-songwriter John Legend performed together at the Grammy Awards on February 12, 2017.

said Wells about the process. "She's not the kind of artist where she takes a song, sings somebody else's music and lyrics and then doesn't think about it again. She cares about every step, and that's what's been so gratifying about this."[6]

When *Ch. 1 Vs. 1* was finished, it featured a compilation of R&B, pop, and inspirational songs about everything from love and heartbreak to family connections and being socially aware in a complicated world. The lead single, "The Good," celebrates and reflects on the love that's possible between two Black women. The acoustic "Sweet Sarah" describes a woman in search of her life's calling. "Tears" explores the beauty of connections with strangers. "I wouldn't say there's a specific genre [for the album], but that is really aligned with Cynthia," said Wells. "The common thread is her—it's her, and it's her voice on this album, and it's her heart."[7]

On September 17, 2021, *Ch. 1 Vs. 1* was released to the world. It reached No. 44 on *Billboard*'s Top Current Album Sales chart. A month later, it rose to No. 77 on the overall Top Album Sales chart.[8]

Though the album didn't do as well as she had hoped, Erivo still felt pleased and relieved to finally get her songs out into the world. "I think the real success of this would be if people listen to this music and see a little bit of themselves in it and are able to have a conversation they haven't been able to have before," she said. "If people can keep connecting to the words and the lyrics and the music in this, then I will feel really, really accomplished."[9]

"YOU'RE NOT HERE"

One of the songs on *Ch. 1 Vs. 1* is titled "You're Not Here." It's about the grief people experience when they lose a friend or loved one. Erivo wrote it to try to come to terms with her relationship with her absent father. "This was just—it was a little moment for me where I had to admit at that time that I was feeling hurt, but then I needed to sort of let go of that," she told NPR. "And the best way for me to let it go was just to sing it, to write it, because then I got the chance to move on."[10]

WRITING FOR KIDS

Hot on the heels of her debut solo album release, Erivo ticked off another accomplishment: publishing a children's book called *Remember to Dream, Ebere*. Released just a week after her record, the picture book features beautiful illustrations by Charnelle Pinkney Barlow.

It is the story of a mother who tells her daughter every night before she goes to bed to make her dreams as big as possible. Erivo spoke to *Harper's Bazaar* about what inspired her book. "I have two goddaughters and a lot of my friends have kids," she said. "I wanted to write something for them and anyone who needs encouragement and wants to know their dreams are valid."[11]

"In storytelling, chapter one and verse one is the way you always begin, and because I believe I'm a storyteller, that's what I wanted to do with my music."[12]

—Cynthia Erivo, 2021

The book garnered many positive reviews. *Publishers Weekly* praised its depiction of supportive parenting that inspires children to chase their dreams. *Variety* highlighted the book's positive message of optimism that it passes on while also entertaining readers.

But the book's biggest praise came from its readers. One fan on the website Goodreads wrote, "This book is pure beauty. The beauty not only comes from the vivid illustrations, but also the calm and loving relationship

Erivo read *Remember to Dream, Ebere* to children in New York City.

of the mother and her daughter Ebere, and the wholesomeness that vibrates from the pages."[13]

For Erivo, *Remember to Dream, Ebere* was a milestone achievement and also a very public way to celebrate her family. The book's inspiration came from Erivo's mother and the support she had given Erivo throughout her life. *Ebere* is also Erivo's sister's middle name. While doing press for the book's release, Erivo read it aloud in a video for Storyline Online, a children's literacy program that produces videos of celebrities reading children's books.

After finishing the read-aloud, Erivo looked at the camera and spoke directly to her audience. "This little book is to celebrate you," she said. "I wrote it for you so that when someone tells you to think a little smaller, tells you to be quiet, to be less bold, to fit in, you come back here to this little book and my words and remember to dream big, big, gargantuan dreams in the brightest colors. Because without you and your big dreams, this world would cry. We need you because you are special."[14]

MOVING ON UP

With her first solo album and picture book under her belt and acting opportunities increasing as the COVID-19 pandemic became less severe, Erivo started accepting more roles again. Throughout 2022 and 2023, she continued to pack her schedule with as

PINOCCHIO'S BLUE FAIRY

In 2022, Erivo starred in the live-action, CG-animated retelling of Walt Disney's *Pinocchio*, directed by Robert Zemeckis. She played the role of the Blue Fairy, the magical creature who brings the puppet Pinocchio to life by singing "When You Wish Upon a Star." Aside from getting to wear a glittery costume and carry a wand, Erivo loved the part because she could relate to the song's message of fearlessly chasing one's dreams.

The original *Luther* series, starring Idris Elba, *left*, premiered on May 4, 2010.

many opportunities as she could handle. In 2022, she appeared as the Blue Fairy in Disney's live-action remake of *Pinocchio*. In 2023, she starred in the Netflix crime thriller *Luther: The Fallen Sun*, a film continuation of the crime drama series *Luther*, starring Idris Elba. She plays a detective who is also Luther's archrival.

"I have never seen anything like her," Erivo said of her role in the movie. "She has this propensity for

Drift was directed by Anthony Chen, *center*, and costarred Alia Shawkat, *left*.

darkness and light. When you meet her, she is very rules-oriented, and she believes in doing the best she can and being on the right side of the law. And when it comes down to it, there are things that she has to do that don't necessarily align with her moral compass."[15]

Also in 2023, Erivo started filming for *Drift*, a movie she produced and starred in about a young Liberian refugee named Jacqueline who escapes her war-torn country to find peace and safety on a Greek island. She signed on to the project because she felt inspired by her mother's experience as a refugee during the Nigerian Civil War (1967–1970). Though the movie didn't get positive reviews overall when it was released in early 2024, many critics praised Erivo's performance.

CHAPTER SEVEN

WICKED

By the end of 2023, Erivo's career was still moving steadily onward and upward. To usher in the holiday season, she booked a few shows at the prestigious Kennedy Center alongside other performers. On December 27, she sang "Alfie" as a tribute to pop-soul legend Dionne Warwick at the Kennedy Center Honors event. On December 31, she rang in the New Year at the Kennedy Center by singing with Ben Platt and Joaquina Kalukango.

But for Erivo, the most exciting next step in her career was coming in 2024. Back in 2021, she had received word that she had landed what many actresses would consider a dream role. She would be playing Elphaba in the film adaptation of the musical *Wicked.* An unofficial prequel to the book *The Wonderful Wizard of Oz,* the musical is based on a

***Wicked* director Jon M. Chu said that he was impressed by how Erivo reinterpreted the character of Elphaba.** >>

1995 novel by Gregory McGuire that imagines the earlier lives of the Wicked Witch Elphaba and the Good Witch Glinda. The film was slated to be released in two parts scheduled for 2024 and 2025. She would costar with Ariana Grande, who was cast as Glinda. Other cast members included Jonathan Bailey, Ethan Slater, Bowen Yang, Michelle Yeoh, and Peter Dinklage.

WICKED ON BROADWAY

The film *Wicked* is based on a play by the same name. The play premiered in San Francisco in 2003. After mixed reviews and a reworking of the score, it then moved to Broadway in October 2003. The Broadway production bewitched audiences thanks to a score by Stephen Schwartz and show-stopping performances by Idina Menzel as Elphaba and Kristin Chenoweth as Glinda. In 2005, the show launched its first US tour. A year later, the show opened in London's West End. In 2025, *Wicked* was still running in the West End and on Broadway.

Getting cast as Elphaba wasn't an assured thing for Erivo, however. Even in the stage musical, the role of Elphaba had rarely gone to a Black actress. For that reason, Erivo almost didn't audition.

Eventually, she decided to go for it rather than let her doubts get the best of her. She remembers how much emotion she had put into the audition. She was astounded and grateful when she learned that her effort had led to her getting the part.

GETTING PHYSICAL IN THE ROLE

From the moment Erivo started rehearsals for *Wicked*, she felt connected to the music. In fact, long before she got the part of Elphaba, she had listened to the songs in *Wicked* and memorized most of the lyrics. The first time she can remember hearing them was when she was a student at RADA. Her friend would play songs from *Wicked* on the piano whenever she was having a bad day. By graduation, she was familiar with the entire musical.

But knowing the lyrics by heart and singing them while doing her own stunts were two very different things. To prepare for the role, Erivo had to engage all parts of her body, not just her voice. For example, she had to learn how to breathe while singing and performing stunts on set. "Instead of using just the front part of my body and my lungs, I could access my back and my sides, to create more space in my body for breath," she said.[1]

> **"To play this role has been one of the roles of a lifetime, to be honest. And it's very exciting and fun and wild and heart-wrenching."**[2]
>
> **—Cynthia Erivo, 2024**

She started training again, both with her vocal coach from *Genius: Aretha* and with an acrobatic trainer. Many mornings, she ran on a treadmill while belting out

Erivo has related to the character of Elphaba ever since she saw a performance of *Wicked*.

Wicked lyrics. For the climactic number, “Defying Gravity,” she had to sing at full volume while strapped into a harness and flying through the air. She wanted to be sure she wouldn’t stumble.

“The first time you do it, it’s a completely out-of-body experience because you have to marry both things up at the same time,” she said. “What the voice is doing and what the body is doing and they’re going in different directions. But when you find out what the balance is and you finally manage to make it work, you finally make the breath work with your body movement and then you make the song and the sound work, it's a really thrilling feeling."[3]

Erivo also had to learn to sit still, sometimes for hours at a time. The character Elphaba has green skin, and applying the paint to Erivo's face and body took four hours or more, plus time for the hair stylist to do her hair. Instead of allowing the film's creators to use computer-generated imagery (CGI) to portray the appearance of her green skin, Erivo purposefully chose to go through the lengthy daily makeup routine because she wanted the experience to feel authentic.

"I knew that if I looked at myself and didn't see the green, I don't think I could have made the connection to Elphaba as much as I did," she said in NBC's *Defying Gravity: The Curtain Rises on Wicked* documentary. "And something happens when all of that green is on, the freckles go on, and the hair goes on, the makeup goes on, the eyes go on, and it's not me I'm looking at. It's her."[4]

Other modifications to Erivo's body were made as well. These included prosthetic ears that covered up her piercings and drawn-on eyebrows. She chose the color of her eye contacts and lipstick too. "We went through four different contact [lenses] and colors, but we wanted the one that would allow people in more," she said.

"I communicate a lot with my eyes, and so we had to find the right shade of green. And we didn't want anything that pushed anyone too far away, but something that was different enough."[5]

EMOTIONAL RESONANCE

For Erivo, becoming Elphaba wasn't just a physical transformation. It was an emotional journey as well. She identified with the way Elphaba felt out of place because of the color of her skin and brought those feelings to the role.

"I understand what it feels like to feel different, to feel like you don't fit. And so I was actually really grateful for the opportunity to play a role like this that would allow, I guess, a little bit of healing, a little bit of understanding, a little bit of reckoning with the things that I've sort

Erivo and costar Ariana Grande became close friends during the production and release of *Wicked*.

of walked through, the experiences that I've had and the times when I've had to navigate a room that doesn't necessarily want me there," she said. "And I think hopefully it'll speak to a lot of people who feel like they are othered and they feel like they don't quite fit in the rooms that they walk into, Black or otherwise, to be honest."[6]

"DEFYING GRAVITY"

At the conclusion of *Wicked*, Erivo belts out the lyrics to "Defying Gravity" while flying through the air. After debuting at No. 2 on the *Billboard* Top Movie Songs chart in November 2024, the song moved up a notch to No. 1 in December and stayed there through January 2025. Fans loved the song so much that they started singing it to Erivo every time they ran into her in person. In an appearance on *Jimmy Kimmel Live*, she said that she considered her fans' behavior to be a sign that she had evoked powerful emotions with her performance.

Erivo also developed deep connections with the *Wicked* cast and crew, especially her costar, Ariana Grande. They practiced their lines every day, sang songs together, and discussed their career aspirations and what they wanted from their lives in general, on and off set. They even got matching tattoos: the words *For good* on their palms and small letters on their ankles. Ariana has *E* for Elphaba and Erivo, and Erivo has *G* for Glinda and Grande.

"I think I've been moved by how much we've grown together. We found a connection almost immediately, when we knew we were going to be doing this together," Erivo said. She continued:

> *It's a very intimate, vulnerable thing to be able to do with another person, which is to sing . . . our relationship has grown and grown and grown and we've fostered and allowed for a really honest, caring relationship. We talk to each other every day, from the moment we were doing this film to today. And I think that has allowed us to really take care of each other on this crazy, wonderful ride that we're on.*[7]

BLOCKBUSTER STATUS

On November 22, 2024, *Wicked* released in theaters. Movie and musical theater lovers flocked to the cinema to see this magical film adaptation come to life. The film's numbers reveal its enormous success. Within a month of its release, *Wicked* had become the highest-grossing movie adaptation of a stage musical in history, making an estimated $114 million at the US box office.[8]

Critics and fans alike praised the film for its larger-than-life special effects, its engaging storyline, and its glowing performances by Grande and Erivo. "Erivo is terrific, her rich, velvety voice cracking under the weight of rejections and ridicule suffered by Elphaba; her eyes showing the bruises that her skin cannot," wrote *The Guardian*'s film critic.[9]

The film, Erivo, and the rest of the cast and crew were nominated for a variety of awards, including Golden Globe Awards, NAACP Image Awards, Screen Actors Guild Awards, Critics' Choice Awards, and others. *Wicked* received ten Academy Award nominations, including Best Motion Picture of the Year.

Erivo herself picked up several award nominations for her portrayal of Elphaba, including a Golden Globe and an Oscar. This second Best Actress Oscar nomination made Erivo only the second Black actress after Viola Davis to be nominated for the award more than once. Following the news of her Oscar nomination, Erivo posted on Instagram,

> *Moments like this don't come along very often, and when they do, it is sacrilege to let them pass by without a moment of gratitude. I am grateful,*

HASTY PUDDING WOMAN OF THE YEAR

On February 5, 2025, Erivo was honored as 2025 Woman of the Year by Harvard University's Hasty Pudding Theatricals. Started in 1844, the group is the world's third-oldest theater club still in operation. In celebration of the event, a parade graced the streets of Harvard Square. Erivo drove through in a green Bentley. Harvard students expressed their delight that Erivo agreed to attend the event.

Erivo sang during the opening of the 97th annual Oscars.

grateful to @theacademy, grateful to be a part of something that makes people feel seen, grateful to be a cog in the wheel of a piece that makes us believe in magic, grateful to have experienced a dream come true, and deeply, deeply grateful for this unbelievable recognition.[10]

The new batch of nominations brought Erivo's total to more than 100 award nominations over the course of her career. She was already looking forward to the release of the second installment of the film in 2025, when the plot turns darker and Elphaba and Glinda go their separate ways as Elphaba rebels against the Wizard of Oz and slowly transforms into the Wicked Witch of the West. Erivo even co-wrote a song for the movie's second chapter. She said in an interview that audiences should expect a tearjerker about Elphaba's deepest self.

CHAPTER EIGHT

FASHION ICON AND PERSONAL LIFE

From the stage to the screen, Erivo has become a superstar beloved by many fans all over the world. She is an award-winning actress and an accomplished musician. As *Glamour* reporter Josh Smith put it, "It's safe to say that Cynthia hasn't just carved out a space for herself or just taken a seat at the table, she's constructed a whole table for herself in an industry that hasn't always made space for her."[1]

For Erivo, becoming as famous as she is meant being smart about the roles she chose to play and feeling confident about what she had to offer. "I just decided that I didn't want to be boxed in. . . . I knew that I wanted to sing, so I thought, 'If I'm going to sing,

Erivo spoke at a 2025 award ceremony held by *Essence* magazine. >>

I'm going to sing in front of as many people as I can, and I'll do it my way,'" she told *Glamour.* "And when it came to playing roles, I knew that I wanted to play a whole gamut of different people. What I'm interested in when it comes to screen or stage is whether or not I have met this person before. If I have met this person before or have played this person before, I'm not interested in doing it again."[2]

But in addition to her life as a celebrated actress and singer, Erivo has other aspects of her identity that she finds just as rewarding. From fashion to fitness to romance and beyond, she tries to keep her life as well-rounded as possible. And when her heart tells her to try something new, she rarely turns away from that feeling.

FASHIONISTA

The older she gets, the more confident Erivo is at expressing herself in flashy styles and equally eye-catching accessories. She is known for her septum piercing and her intricately designed long, pointy nails, which have featured everything from Vincent van Gogh's painting *Starry Night* to Michelangelo's *The Creation of Adam* reimagined with Black women. Because of her short stature, she loves wearing attention-grabbing platform heels.

She says her style is "not because I want to make a statement for other people. It's what I feel like on the day. Sometimes it's understated and monochromatic . . . sometimes it's really bright and colorful. . . . It's like armor. I like being a small person, but I think there's something about clothes that can take up a little bit of room."[3]

WICKED FASHIONABLE

To the fashion press and her many fans, Erivo is one of the best-dressed stars out there. Her red carpet choices for *Wicked* showcased her willingness to make bold choices and have fun while doing it. At the Los Angeles premiere of the film, she wore a bright green Louis Vuitton dress with cutouts at the sides and front and a giant matching wrap made of green fringe. At the 2025 Oscars ceremony, Erivo fully embraced her witchy look once again. She wore a dark green velvet Louis Vuitton gown with exaggerated hips and shoulders and a pointed collar to honor Oz and classical Hollywood fashion.

Throughout her career, Erivo has had plenty of show-stopping red carpet moments, enough to earn her a reputation as one of the industry's most fashionable stars. At the 2017 Grammy Awards, she wore a midnight blue, textured, strapless Luisa Beccaria gown with a velvet bodice to complement her bleached-blond hair. For the 2019 Tony Awards, she wore a sleek, white gown with a slit up the side and an array of yellow and white feathers along the leg and shoulders. Her Louis Vuitton dress for

At the 2025 SAG Awards, Erivo wore green nails to reference her role in *Wicked*.

the 2023 British Academy of Film and Television Arts (BAFTA) Awards featured dozens of seemingly glowing red, orange, and gold shards and a train that stretched out from the back.

One of the most statement-making pieces was her dress for the 2025 SAG Awards. Her longtime stylist Jason Bolden found a woven, silver dress with bell sleeves and a fringed high collar from Alexander McQueen's fall 1997 couture collection for Givenchy. "You have this one woman of color who is giving you what the fashion world and all these people would say is quintessential amazingness," he said of their longtime collaboration on award-night fashion. "Every time she's hitting the carpet it's custom, it's couture, it's new, it's fresh and pure red carpet energy."[4]

FITNESS GURU

Throughout her career, Erivo has become known for her distinctive, one-of-a-kind choices when it comes to fashion. But beyond her fancy nails and red-carpet looks, she has made it a priority to stay healthy too. In 2018, she revealed that has embraced a vegan diet and cooks plant-based meals for herself to ensure her body is getting the right nutrients. She also carries gummy vitamins with her wherever she goes.

When she's traveling, she stays true to her diet even when she's constantly on the move. "I travel with seaweed chips, edamame chips, tea, peanut butter, avocados," she told *Bon Appetit*. "I always make a meal for the flight I'm going to be on that day and carry it in a thermos. I always have nuts and apples. If I'm in a hotel, I always ask them to make sure [to] have a kettle and a fridge."[5]

Erivo also exercises frequently, even when faced with a busy schedule. She runs often, sometimes as much as nine miles (14 km) every other day. She has run the SHAPE Women's Half Marathon twice and plans to run marathons in Belgium and Paris. At the 2022 London Marathon, she beat her own record with a personal-best time of three hours, 35 minutes, and 36 seconds. She also does Pilates, yoga, indoor cycling, barre, weight training, and full-body exercises, including squats, lunges, push-ups, and pull-ups.

"[Exercise] is the thing that keeps my brain working. Otherwise, I start flagging halfway through the day," she says. "I'd rather get up early, get a workout in, and be able to move through the day, [than] struggle halfway through the day because I haven't taken the time to work for myself."[6]

When she isn't working or exercising, Erivo has other hobbies. She tries to use social media for positive reasons. She knits and drinks peppermint tea. She plays with her two dogs, Gigi and Caleb. In quiet moments, she lights a candle and reads or listens to jazz records. And she tries to maintain an upbeat attitude whenever possible.

ERIVO'S WORKOUT ESSENTIALS

Erivo's workouts have varied over the years. But she does have a general routine she tries to practice when running, lifting weights, doing yoga, or cycling. First, she picks out her workout outfit. Then, she grabs a glass of ice-cold water. Finally, she chooses her workout music, ranging from Erykah Badu and Jill Scott to Yebba and Beyoncé. Staying fit makes her feel happy. "The one thing that happens after you work out is that you get sort of a rush of endorphins and those things help to alleviate stress and they make you happier," she says. "So, I think that it's a knock-on effect of working out that, essentially, my life is happier because I'm working out."[7]

Erivo's finish time at the 2022 London Marathon was more than 20 minutes faster than her previous personal best time.

She explains that by giving herself small gifts every day, she avoids feeling depleted at the end of each week or month. Instead, she always feels whole.

FEARLESS ROMANTIC

Throughout her prolific career, Erivo has been open about her love of fashion and fitness. But one area where she's more private is her romantic life. In fact, not much was written about it in the press until 2021. She reportedly dated British actor Dean John-Wilson starting in 2013. The two met while they were working on the theater production of *Sister Act*. They made their red-carpet debut in 2016, when he was playing the lead in the West End production of Disney's *Aladdin*.

Erivo then dated actor and musician Mario Martinez for around two years, from 2017 to 2019. Also during that time, in 2018, Erivo connected with actress, producer, and screenwriter Lena Waithe at the Met Gala. After that party, she was occasionally seen with Waithe, sparking rumors about a possible romantic relationship. As Waithe described it to *Variety*,

> *The first time I met her was at the Met Gala, which is where all the cool kids go to meet each other. I had seen her in* The Color Purple *twice . . . I remember seeing her on TV . . . [and] I remember [thinking], 'Who is this tiny person with a British accent?' . . . We've just been vibing ever since.*[8]

Finally, in 2021 and 2022, she came out to the public as queer in a series of articles published in *The Standard* and *British Vogue*. In them, she said she wanted to be more honest about all the aspects of her life that made her who she is as a person. "I could feel myself actively hiding that part of myself and it didn't feel good. That takes a lot of energy to uphold and there is zero return," she said in *British Vogue*. "I felt like I was looking at my community be alive and vibrant from inside a glass box. I don't want to watch from inside that glass box anymore. . . . There's not enough room in there and there is no ventilation!"[9]

Erivo prefers to keep the details of her romantic life private from the probing eyes of the public. "I'm very tight-lipped with my relationships, 'cause I don't think that my relationship is for anyone else but for me . . . I spend so much of my life sharing everything—whether it's my work or my soul or my life in speeches. I think I give enough of myself that I'm allowed to keep something for me," she told *Vanity Fair*. "It's enough for people to know that I'm a queer person who could have relationships with men or women or neither."[10]

ROLE MODEL

Whether she's singing or acting, showing off her latest outfit at an awards ceremony, or performing at a sold-out concert, Erivo says one of the most rewarding aspects of being so successful is that she has become a role model

Erivo spoke at the GLAAD Media Awards on March 27, 2025. GLAAD is a nonprofit organization that advocates for fair representation of queer people in media.

During her Stonewall Day performance, Erivo covered songs by Whitney Houston and Sinéad O'Connor.

for kids. She has a special affinity for young Black girls who say they feel lost or out of place in their environment. Through her actions and her words, she insists that the key to gaining confidence is to embrace one's true self no matter what.

For Erivo, a 2024 interview with nine-year-old Isabelle from *Cocoa Girl* was the perfect opportunity to help make a shy kid feel more special. Isabelle asked Erivo if she ever felt different over the course of her life. Erivo's response was telling. "I think I've always felt different. . . . When I was younger, it was very hard . . . because I didn't really fit in, and now I don't really fit in, but I kind of like it. I think I'm OK with that," she said. "It takes time to get used to how different you are, and it takes time to feel confident in it, but I think you're beautiful as you are. I think that all the differences that you have make you really, really special."[11]

One way that Erivo models good behavior for younger fans is by supporting charitable efforts and organizations. She has appeared at numerous events to speak or fundraise for causes she believes in. She has also performed for charity.

On June 28, 2024, Erivo headlined a benefit concert at Stonewall Day, an event that commemorates a series of demonstrations that occurred near New York City's Stonewall Inn in 1969 following a long pattern of police violence against queer people in the surrounding neighborhood. The money raised by the concert went toward the Stonewall National Monument Visitor Center, an official unit of the National Park Service.

That November, Erivo joined actor David Oyelowo in leading a keynote discussion at a fundraiser held by the Godwin, Ebele, Afam, Nche & Nma, and Chukwugozie Onyema (GEANCO) Foundation. This organization provides medical and educational services and funding for Nigerians in need. Some of the money raised at this event went to the GEANCO Foundation's David Oyelowo Leadership Scholarship for Girls. This program identifies young Nigerian women suffering from socio-economic circumstances and provides them with tuition, health care, and other services.

PUTTING IT ALL TOGETHER

In 2025, Erivo's career was at an all-time high. At the 2025 Oscars ceremony in March, she was honored by the Academy and performed a show-stopping duet with costar Ariana Grande. She hosted the Tony Awards at Radio City Music Hall in New York City on June 8. And in November, *Wicked: For Good* was planned for release in theaters worldwide.

Erivo had many more projects scheduled for release in 2025 too. She appeared in the second season of *Poker Face*, Peacock's critically acclaimed series from creator Rian Johnson starring Natasha Lyonne. She voiced a character called The Slink in the Disney Junior animated series *Robogobo*.

In November 2024, it was reported that Erivo's production company, Edith's Daughter, signed a first-look deal with Universal Pictures. In this type of entertainment industry agreement, a producer or creator gives a studio the exclusive right to review and potentially develop their new projects first. "Cynthia's world-class talent is matched only by her unwavering commitment to authenticity, representation, and empathy as a storyteller," said Universal Pictures president Peter Cramer. "She has inspired us all throughout the making of *Wicked*, and we are so honored that she has chosen to partner with Universal to help amplify her mission at Edith's Daughter."[12]

While all that was going on, Erivo was also working on a new, even more personal solo album that was partly autobiographical. Already a star in the music world in her own right, Grande helped Erivo navigate the ins and outs of the music industry to make the record the best it could be. The album, titled *I Forgive You*, was released on June 6, 2025. Critics gave it positive reviews; one writer for *Variety* praised Erivo's low-key vocals that nevertheless grip the listener's attention.

Above all, Erivo was more excited than ever about her prospects in the future. She would continue to teach the

ERIVO'S FAVORITES

In 2021, Erivo was interviewed by *Harper's Bazaar UK*. In the interview, she listed off a few of her favorite things. One of her favorite books is Cicely Tyson's memoir, *Just as I Am*. One of her all-time favorite films is *The Devil Wears Prada*. The song that will always get her dancing is "Raspberry Beret" by Prince. Her favorite dance move is the two-step. Gummy bears are a favorite snack.

next generation of talent at RADA. She would jump at the chance to work with Grande again. And she hoped to direct a film or TV series one day if the right opportunity came along. "I haven't done it before. But that's never really been a reservation for me," she told *AnOther* magazine in 2025. "I've really enjoyed watching directors. I'm curious when I'm on sets. I love asking questions. I love discovering and understanding what's going on and how things work. And if that wasn't a passion that kept coming up, I would know it wasn't for me."[13]

Whatever the next step would be, Erivo felt more than ready to embrace the unknown. "When I think about the next milestone, I'm not entirely sure what it will be," she admitted. But looking forward, staying focused and positive, and being the best actress, musician, singer, person she can be is what will get her there.

"You don't necessarily have to wait for someone to see who you are to be celebrated," Erivo told *Essence*. "You can step into yourself and into what you think might be your destiny. You can be all of who you are—and take the time to discover what that is. . . . If you keep showing up, if you keep being who you are, eventually no one can really question it."[14]

Erivo blew a kiss at the BAFTA Film Awards on February 16, 2025.

ESSENTIAL FACTS

Full Name: Cynthia Chinasaokwu Onyedinmanasu Amarachukwu Owezuke Echimino Erivo

Date of Birth: January 8, 1987

Place of Birth: London, England

Parents: Edith Erivo; her father's name is not publicly known

Education: La Retraite Roman Catholic Girls' School, University of East London, Royal Academy of Dramatic Art

RISE TO STARDOM

- Cynthia Erivo trained in acting and singing at the Royal Academy of Dramatic Art.
- After college, Erivo starred as Celie in a production of *The Color Purple* on London's West End from 2013 to 2015.
- In 2015, Erivo moved to the United States to play the role of Celie on Broadway in New York City.
- After wrapping up her role in the Broadway revival of *The Color Purple*, Erivo began to take film roles.

CAREER HIGHLIGHTS

- For her role in *The Color Purple*, Erivo won a Tony Award, a Grammy Award, and a Daytime Emmy Award.
- In addition to acting, Erivo published a children's picture book, *Remember to Dream, Ebere*, in 2021.
- Erivo released her debut album, *Ch. 1 Vs. 1*, in 2021.
- In 2024, Erivo's performance in *Wicked* earned her an Academy Award nomination for Best Actress in a Leading Role.

MAJOR PLAYS AND FILMS

- *The Color Purple* (2013, 2015)
- *Widows* (2018)
- *Harriet* (2019)
- *Genius: Aretha* (2021)
- *Wicked* (2024)
- *Wicked: For Good* (2025)

QUOTE

"I don't believe that many things are impossible to achieve so long as you put your mind to it and take the time to get it done."

—Cynthia Erivo, 2017

GLOSSARY

abolitionist
A person who wants to end slavery.

agent
A person who represents an actress or actor and is in charge of getting them auditions for parts.

biopic
A biographical movie.

cabaret
A form of entertainment that showcases the talents of many different performers, such as singers and dancers.

camaraderie
A feeling of friendliness or goodwill toward other people in a group.

debut
The first time an actor, musician, or artist performs in a certain role or releases a certain product, such as an album.

dialect
A regional variety of language with distinct vocabulary, grammar, and accent.

diminutive
The state of being very small.

discrimination
Unfair treatment of other people, usually because of race, age, or gender.

gala
A public celebration marking an occasion.

prestigious
Honored or highly praised.

prosthetic
An artificial body part used for special effects in movies and theater.

queer
Relating to or being a person who is not heterosexual or cisgender.

quintessential
Perfectly representative of a particular kind of person or thing.

rapturously
In a way that shows overwhelming emotion or passion.

red carpet
An event before an awards show where performers or celebrities show up in gorgeous attire, get photographed, and do interviews.

refugee
A person who flees their country to escape danger or persecution.

undeterred
Not discouraged or prevented from acting.

wallowing
Behaving as if helpless.

ADDITIONAL RESOURCES

SELECTED BIBLIOGRAPHY

Frazier, Rozalynn S. "The Power of Cynthia Erivo." *Shape*, 8 Mar. 2023, shape.com. Accessed 3 Mar. 2025.

Gross, Terry. "'Genius' Actor Cynthia Erivo Opens Up Her Voice on *Ch. 1 Vs. 1*." *National Public Radio*, 18 Oct. 2021, npr.org. Accessed 3 Mar. 2025.

Murphy, Chris. "*Wicked* Stars Cynthia Erivo and Ariana Grande on Love, Defying Rumors, and Flying High." *Vanity Fair*, 30 Sept. 2024, vanityfair.com. Accessed 3 Mar. 2025.

Williams, Zoe. "Cynthia Erivo on Fame, Fear and Not Fitting In," *Guardian*, 27 Jan. 2025, theguardian.com. Accessed 3 Mar. 2025.

FURTHER READINGS

Edwards, Sue Bradford. *Ariana Grande*. Abdo, 2026.

Hartwell, Eva. *Acting for Teens*. Oak Harbor, 2023.

Murray, Laura K. *Making Movies*. Abdo, 2025.

ONLINE RESOURCES

To learn more about Cynthia Erivo, please visit **abdobooklinks.com** or scan this QR code. These links are routinely monitored and updated to provide the most current information available.

MORE INFORMATION

For more information on this subject, contact or visit the following organizations:

ACADEMY MUSEUM OF MOTION PICTURES

6067 Wilshire Blvd.
Los Angeles, CA 90036
academymuseum.org/en

The Academy Museum of Motion Pictures is the largest museum in the United States devoted to the art and science of moviemaking. It features film screenings and interactive displays about many of the world's greatest movies.

NATIONAL MUSEUM OF AFRICAN AMERICAN HISTORY AND CULTURE

1400 Constitution Ave. NW
Washington, DC 20560
nmaahc.si.edu

The National Museum of African American History has hosted hundreds of interactive exhibits and film screenings about some of the most influential people and cultural moments in US history, including Alice Walker and *The Color Purple*, Aretha Franklin, Harriet Tubman and the Underground Railroad, and more.

ROYAL ACADEMY OF DRAMATIC ART (RADA)

62-64 Gower St.
London, England WC1E 6ED
rada.ac.uk

In existence for more than 100 years, RADA is one of the top performing arts schools in the world. It provides training in acting, stage managing, singing, and stagecraft.

SOURCE NOTES

CHAPTER 1. REACHING FOR THE SPOTLIGHT

1. Penny Wrenn. "Cynthia Erivo Makes 'The Color Purple' Broadway All Her Own." *Essence*, 27 Oct. 2020, essence.com. Accessed 30 May 2025.

2. Faith Fancher. "Men Are Not the Center of Alice Walker's Universe." *NPR*, 3 July 1983, npr.org. Accessed 30 May 2025.

3. Frank DiLella. "NY1 Online: Cynthia Erivo Reacts to 2016 Tony Nomination." *Spectrum News NY 1*, 3 May 2023, spectrumlocalnews.com. Accessed 30 May 2025.

4. "70th Annual Tony Awards The Color Purple 2016." *YouTube*. Uploaded by Darnell Bennett, 3 Sept. 2016, youtube.com. Accessed 30 May 2025.

5. "2016 Tonys Red Carpet: Cynthia Erivo." *Facebook*. Uploaded by Tony Awards, 24 June 2016, facebook.com. Accessed 30 May 2025.

6. Allison P. Davis. "A Star Is Born." *Vulture*, June 2017, vulture.com. Accessed 30 May 2025.

7. "Acceptance Speech: Cynthia Erivo - Best Leading Actress in a Musical (2016)." *YouTube*. Uploaded by BroadwayInHD, 12 Apr. 2017, youtube.com. Accessed 30 May 2025.

8. "Cynthia Erivo's Message to Her Future Self from the First Day of Filming Wicked." *YouTube*. Uploaded by BAFTA, 23 Dec. 2024, youtube.com. Accessed 30 May 2025.

CHAPTER 2. A STAR IS BORN

1. Mary Florence Bello. "Women of the Year Awards Music: Cynthia Erivo." *Harper's Bazaar*, 3 Nov. 2021, harpersbazaar.com. Accessed 30 May 2025.

2. Terry Gross. "'Genius' Actor Cynthia Erivo Opens Up Her Voice on 'Ch. 1 Vs. 1.'" *NPR*, 18 Oct. 2021, npr.org. Accessed 30 May 2025.

3. Gross, "'Genius' Actor Cynthia Erivo Opens Up Her Voice."

4. Zoe Williams. "Cynthia Erivo on Fame, Fear and Not Fitting In: 'I've Never Talked about How Tough My Journey Has Been.'" *Guardian*, 27 Jan. 2025, theguardian.com. Accessed 30 May 2025.

5. Williams, "Cynthia Erivo on Fame, Fear and Not Fitting In."

6. Williams, "Cynthia Erivo on Fame, Fear and Not Fitting In."

7. Michael Paulson. "The Actress Cynthia Erivo Rises with 'The Color Purple.'" *New York Times*, 22 Dec. 2015, nytimes.com. Accessed 30 May 2025.

8. Williams, "Cynthia Erivo on Fame, Fear and Not Fitting In."

CHAPTER 3. CLIMBING THE ROPES

1. Rozalynn S. Frazier. "The Power of Cynthia Erivo." *Shape*, 8 Mar. 2023, shape.com. Accessed 30 May 2025.

2. Jonathan Baz. "Cynthia Erivo—London's Rising Star—Now, by Royal Invitation." *Jonathan Baz Reviews*, 16 Feb. 2014, jonathanbaz.com. Accessed 30 May 2025.

3. "Cynthia Erivo: Eight Things We Learned from Her This Cultural Life Interview." *BBC*, n.d., bbc.co.uk. Accessed 30 May 2025.

4. Isabelle Casey. "Exclusive: Why Cynthia Erivo's School Teachers 'Always Knew' She Would be a Hollywood Star." *Hello!*, 7 Jan. 2025, hellomagazine.com. Accessed 30 May 2025.

5. Baz, "Cynthia Erivo—London's Rising Star."

CHAPTER 4. A BIG MOVE PAYS OFF

1. "Cynthia Erivo on How 'The Color Purple' Paved Her Way to Broadway." *YouTube*. Uploaded by Peacock, 4 July 2024, youtube.com. Accessed 30 May 2025.

2. Michael Gioia. "Cynthia Erivo on How Color Purple Has Changed Her Life." *Playbill*, 25 Dec. 2015, playbill.com. Accessed 30 May 2025.

3. Jesse Green. "Theater Review: The Color Purple Is One of the Greatest Revivals Ever." *Vulture*, 10 Dec. 2015, vulture.com. Accessed 3 May 2025.

4. Nick Weldon. "How 'Wicked' Star Cynthia Erivo Trained for the New York City Marathon." *Runner's World*, 26 Nov. 2024, runnersworld.com. Accessed 30 May 2025.

5. Weldon, "How 'Wicked' Star Cynthia Erivo Trained for the New York City Marathon."

6. Michael Paulson. "The Actress Cynthia Erivo Rises with 'The Color Purple.'" *New York Times*, 22 Dec. 2015, nytimes.com. Accessed 30 May 2025.

7. Meg Walters. "The Stunning Transformation of Cynthia Erivo." *List*, 14 Feb. 2024, thelist.com. Accessed 30 May 2025.

8. Rebecca Schriesheim. "You Need to See Cynthia Erivo's Performance in This Tarantino-Esque Noir Before 'Wicked.'" *Collider*, 23 Nov. 2024, collider.com. Accessed 30 May 2025.

9. Shafiq Najib. "All the Stars Who Have an EGOT and Who Is Close." *ABC 7 Eyewitness News*, 5 Feb. 2025, abc7.com. Accessed 30 May 2025.

10. Gabriela Barkho. "Cynthia Erivo Discusses Her New Project, Serialized Podcast 'Carrier.'" *Observer*, 15 July 2019, observer.com. Accessed 30 May 2025.

11. Nate Jones. "Cynthia Erivo Answers Every Question We Have about Widows." *Vulture*, 30 Oct. 2019, vulture.com. Accessed 30 May 2025.

CHAPTER 5. TWO KNOCKOUT ROLES

1. Reggie Ugwu. "The Hashtag That Changed the Oscars: An Oral History." *New York Times*, 9 Sept. 2020, nytimes.com. Accessed 30 May 2025.

2. Kate Aurthur. "Inside Cynthia Erivo's Journey to Making a 'Badass' Harriet Tubman Biopic." *Variety*, 29 Oct. 2019, variety.com. Accessed 30 May 2025.

3. Aurthur, "Inside Cynthia Erivo's Journey."

4. Aurthur, "Inside Cynthia Erivo's Journey."

5. Cynthia Erivo. "Playing Harriet Tubman Changed My Life." *Guideposts*, n.d., guideposts.org. Accessed 30 May 2025.

6. Erivo, "Playing Harriet Tubman Changed My Life."

7. Aurthur, "Inside Cynthia Erivo's Journey."

8. Meg Walters. "The Stunning Transformation of Cynthia Erivo." *List*, 14 Feb. 2024, thelist.com. Accessed 30 May 2025.

SOURCE NOTES

CHAPTER 6. BRANCHING OUT

1. Louis Wise. "Cynthia Erivo Interview: The Highly Acclaimed Actress's Debut Album Means She's Dancing to Her Own Tune." *Standard*, 27 Aug. 2021, standard.co.uk. Accessed 30 May 2025.

2. Gary Gerard Hamilton. "Cynthia Erivo Is Vulnerable, yet Powerful on 'Ch. 1 Vs. 1.'" *Associated Press*, 29 Sept. 2021, apnews.com. Accessed 30 May 2025.

3. "Cynthia Erivo Reveals the Career Advice Oprah Winfrey Gave Her." *YouTube*. Uploaded by Harper's Bazaar UK, 10 Nov. 2021, youtube.com. Accessed 30 May 2025.

4. Mary Florence Bello. "Women of the Year Awards Music: Cynthia Erivo." *Harper's Bazaar*, 3 Nov. 2021, harpersbazaar.com. Accessed 30 May 2025.

5. Hamilton, "Cynthia Erivo Is Vulnerable, yet Powerful."

6. Hamilton, "Cynthia Erivo Is Vulnerable, yet Powerful."

7. Hamilton, "Cynthia Erivo Is Vulnerable, yet Powerful."

8. Xander Zellner, "Hot 100 First-timers: Cynthia Erivo, Jeff Goldblum & More 'Wicked' Cast Score Their First Chart Entries." *Billboard*, 4 Dec. 2024, billboard.com. Accessed 30 May 2025.

9. Hamilton, "Cynthia Erivo Is Vulnerable, yet Powerful."

10. Michel Martin. "Cynthia Erivo Sings Her Own Words in 1st Solo Album." *NPR*, 25 Sept. 2021, npr.org. Accessed 30 May 2025.

11. Bello, "Women of the Year Awards Music: Cynthia Erivo."

12. D'Shonda Brown. "Cynthia Erivo Announces Debut Album, 'Ch. 1 Vs. 1.'" *Essence*, 4 June 2021, essence.com. Accessed 30 May 2025.

13. Summer Newbold. Review of *Remember to Dream, Ebere*, by Cynthia Erivo. *Goodreads*, 11 Nov. 2021, goodreads.com. Accessed 30 May 2025.

14. "'Remember to Dream, Ebere' Read by Cynthia Erivo." *YouTube*. Uploaded by StorylineOnline, 4 Oct. 2021, youtube.com. Accessed 30 May 2025.

15. Rozalynn S. Frazier. "The Power of Cynthia Erivo." *Shape*, 8 Mar. 2023, shape.com. Accessed 30 May 2025.

CHAPTER 7. *WICKED*

1. "Cynthia Erivo: Eight Things We Learned from Her This Cultural Life Interview." *BBC*, n.d., bbc.co.uk. Accessed 30 May 2025.

2. Meg Walters. "The Stunning Transformation of Cynthia Erivo." *List*, 14 Feb. 2024, thelist.com. Accessed 30 May 2025.

3. Mark Olsen and Yvonne Villarreal. "How 'Wicked' Star Cynthia Erivo Became Elphaba, from 'Defying Gravity' to 'the Perfect Green.'" *Los Angeles Times*, 21 Nov. 2024, latimes.com. Accessed 30 May 2025.

4. Sarah El-Mahmoud. "The Story behind Why Wicked Made Cynthia Erivo's Elphaba Green without CGI: 'Something Happens to the DNA in the Space.'" *Cinemablend*, 25 Mar. 2025, cinemablend.com. Accessed 30 May 2025.

5. Olsen and Villarreal, "How 'Wicked' Star Cynthia Erivo Became Elphaba."

6. Olsen and Villarreal, "How 'Wicked' Star Cynthia Erivo Became Elphaba."

7. Olsen and Villarreal, "How 'Wicked' Star Cynthia Erivo Became Elphaba."

CONTINUED. . .

8. Nicole Fell. "'Wicked: For Good': Here's What We Know about Part 2." *Hollywood Reporter*, 31 Mar. 2025, hollywoodreporter.com. Accessed 30 May 2025.

9. Wendy Ide. "Wicked Review – Cynthia Erivo and Ariana Grande Make the Magic Happen." *Guardian*, 24 Nov. 2024, theguardian.com. Accessed 30 May 2025.

10. Carson Blackwelder and Angeline Jane Bernabe. "Cynthia Erivo Is Closer to an EGOT – Will She Achieve It at the 2025 Oscars?" *ABC News*, 1 Mar. 2025, abcnews.go.com. Accessed 30 May 2025.

CHAPTER 8. FASHION ICON AND PERSONAL LIFE

1. Josh Smith. "Cynthia Erivo: 'I'm Really Proud That I've Come Out, I Feel More Myself than I Ever Have.'" *Glamour*, 8 Nov. 2022, glamourmagazine.co.uk. Accessed 30 May 2025.

2. Smith, "Cynthia Erivo: 'I'm Really Proud That I've Come Out.'"

3. "Cynthia Erivo: Eight Things We Learned from Her This Cultural Life Interview." *BBC*, n.d., bbc.co.uk. Accessed 30 May 2025.

4. Janelle Okwodu. "Stylist Jason Bolden on How Cynthia Erivo Brought Black Joy to the Red Carpet." *Vogue*, 6 Feb. 2020, vogue.com. Accessed 30 May 2025.

5. Claire Saffitz. "Cynthia Erivo on Being a Workout Warrior and Holding Hollywood Accountable." *Bon Appétit*, 29 Jan. 2018, bonappetit.com. Accessed 30 May 2025.

6. Rozalynn S. Frazier. "The Power of Cynthia Erivo." *Shape*, 8 Mar. 2023, shape.com. Accessed 30 May 2025.

7. Vanessa Etienne. "Cynthia Erivo Exercises Every Day for Her Mental Health and Doesn't Set Goals: 'I Like My Body.'" *People*, 10 Nov. 2021, people.com. Accessed 30 May 2025.

8. Mehera Bonner. "Cynthia Erivo and Lena Waithe's Relationship Timeline Is So Low-Key and Sweet." *Cosmopolitan*, 2 Mar. 2025, cosmopolitan.com. Accessed 30 May 2025.

9. Jacqueline Woodson. "'Some Young Black Queer Actress Will Know She's Not Alone': Cynthia Erivo on Changing the Narrative." *British Vogue*, 11 July 2022, vogue.co.uk. Accessed 30 May 2025.

10. Aimée Lutkin. "Cynthia Erivo's Complete Dating History." *Elle*, 4 Mar. 2024, elle.com. Accessed 30 May 2025.

11. "Cocoa Girl Journalist Isabelle Interviews Her Role Model #cynthiaerivo." *YouTube*. Uploaded by Cocoa Kids TV, 23 Nov. 2024, youtube.com. Accessed 30 May 2025.

12. George Lewis. "Cynthia Erivo Lands Huge New Deal following Wicked Success." *Digital Spy*, 23 Nov. 2024, digitalspy.com. Accessed 30 May 2025.

13. Tim Blanks. "How Cynthia Erivo Claimed Her Space in Hollywood, and Held It." *AnOther*, 13 Feb. 2025, anothermag.com. Accessed 30 May 2025.

14. Brande Victorian. "Black Women in Hollywood: Cynthia Erivo." *Essence*, 18 Feb. 2025, essence.com. Accessed 30 May 2025.

INDEX

ABOUT THE AUTHOR

ALEXIS POPI

Alexis Popi has written dozens of articles and more than 50 books for young readers on a variety of topics ranging from current events and biographies of famous people to nutrition and fitness to major milestones in history. She is also a professional book critic with reviews of adult and young adult books, author interviews, and other publishing industry–related articles published in the *New York Times*, the *Washington Post*, the *San Francisco Chronicle*, and more. Alexis is inspired by Cynthia Erivo's power and talent as a singer, actress, and fashion maven. She lives in the Pacific Northwest with her husband, cats, and hundreds of books.